THE GREAT GIFT

THE GREAT GIFT

For someone special

Brock Tully

First Published in Canada 2013 by
Influence Publishing

Book Cover Design: Marla Thompson
Typesetting: Greg Salisbury
Author Photographer: Wilma Fuchs
Artists: Heidi Thompson (Thoughts)
          Christine Moulson (Great Gift Story)

DISCLAIMER: The Great Gift Story is a work of fiction. The
information is of a general nature to inspire readers. Readers
of this publication agree that neither Brock Tully, nor his pub-
lisher will be held responsible or liable for damages that may
be alleged or resulting directly or indirectly from their use of
this publication.

Dedicated to...Gandhi, Martin Luther King, & Winnie-the-Pooh.

TESTIMONIALS

"Brock has created a great piece of insightful, heart-warming, & profound 'sayings' that reconnect us to our heart...it is a unique & special gift for everyone, full of original inspiring 'thoughts'."
Azim Jamal, # 1 best selling co- author of "The Power of Giving"

"Brock Tully is a natural writer with an inordinate sense of life and passion who has written an exceptional book. Simply told, sentimental, and profoundly true... you won't want to put it down..."
Warren Erhart, President and CEO, White Spot Restaurants

"The Great Gift is inspirational gold. Masterfully written, Brock's witty prose and profound perceptions will have you repeatedly laying the book on your lap as you reflect, nod in concurrence and smile."
Joyce M. Ross, Kindness is Key Training Inc.

ACKNOWLEDGMENTS

Much thanks to Beryle Chambers for editing 'The Great Gift' story; Christine Moulson for illustrating "The Great Gift" story; and Heidi Thompson for illustrating the 'Reflections' 'thoughts'.

Contents

Dedication
Testimonials
Acknowledgements
Introduction

Chapter One
Comunicating from the Heart 1

Chapter Two
Being True to Our Heart 27

Chapter Three
The Courage to Follow Our Heart 51

The Great Gift Story 77

Chapter Four
The Determined Heart 101

Chapter Five
The Joyful Heart 121

Chapter Six
The Kind Heart 143

Author Biography 167

Introduction

"The Great Gift... for someone special"

...in 1970 i was very disconnected from my heart, depressed, and close to 'taking my life'. Fortunately, i chose to climb on my old 10-speed bicycle, before people were cross-country cycling and i rode all around the U.S. (33 States) and Mexico - what turned out to be 10,000 miles was most importantly, a short, but slow, 12 inch journey back from my head to my heart....that continues today!

...i'm blessed and grateful that by opening my heart, these little 'thoughts' were able to come out 'through me'. It is very important, to me, that you know that, too often, i lose touch with my heart and i don't live up to what i write....this is my journey. If i waited until i was living perfectly, i would, i'm sure, never publish this book.

...the first 'thought' i ever put to paper, right after my bicycle journey, really got me started on my journey back to my heart...

"...i'd rather be seen
            for who i am
        and be alone...
    than be accepted
            for someone i'm not
        and be lonely."

...since the first bicycle trip, i unconsciously started writing with the small 'i' - i've come to realize that it was my need to get away from the big 'I' that represents, for me, my ego. i was drawn to the small, gentle 'i' that connects me to my heart and the hearts of others.

...i also write my thoughts in the 'i' rather than the 'you' or 'we' because it is important, for me, to share what 'i feel' and to respect that others might feel differently. i write to inspire people to think, care, and smile more!

...i really hope "The Great Gift...for someone special" inspires and touches you and supports you on your journey back to your special heart.

Chapter One:

Communicating from the Heart

...i first started writing little 'thoughts' as a way of listening to, and becoming closer to my heart...i realized that when i love to 'grow', i seem to grow more loving", ...my constant challenge is 'to live' the 'thoughts' i write so that my actions will be a 'reflection' of my heart...

"...i'd rather be seen
            for who i am
      and be alone...
than be accepted
            for someone i'm not
      and be lonely."

"...when we communicate,
we see that
our likenesses
are greater than
our differences...
when we don't communicate,
we're more likely
to 'only' see
our differences."

"...i learn most from you,
　　　　　not when you 'try'
　　　　to teach me...
　but,
　　when you 'are'
　　　what you want me
　　　　　　to know."

"...building walls around me
            takes energy
            and i feel old and tired...
    when i tire
            of building walls
        i have lots of energy,
            and i feel young again."

"...when i'm quick
        to give 'my word'
    and i don't mean it...
it quickly becomes
        just 'a' word
    with no meaning."

"...when you say
        you disagree
    with me...
do you disagree
        that 'i feel' this way,
    or do you disagree
            because 'you feel'
    differently?"

"...when i talk a lot
and i say very little,
people tend
to stop listening...
when i talk little
but say a lot,
people have a tendency
to stop and listen."

"...when i'm confused...
it's better to say
what i'm feeling,
and have it sound confusing,
than to confuse you
by waiting
until i can say it,
better."

"...the more open we are
        the less we seem strangers...
i've known people i've just met
            better than some people
    i've known for years...
i hope we're always open...
        you're too precious
            to be a stranger."

"...i don't want you
            to fill a 'hole'
                        in me...
      i want you
            to feel 'whole'
                        with me."

"...i want you
to be happy
to see me...
but,
i don't want you
to need to see me
for your happiness."

"...the beautiful thing
about saying 'no' to me,
is that when you say 'yes'
i know you really mean it."

"...saying 'no' to me
isn't being mean...
it gives 'yes'
more meaning."

"...i used to 'think'
so hard about
how i thought
i should be...
now i 'am'
so easily
who i want to be."

"...if i take part
           in 'taking apart'
    others
           by gossiping...
others will probably
           gossip about me
    as soon as
           we are apart."

\

"when i argue
          i need to be right...
when i discuss
          i want to share...
i hope my desire
          to love
     is stronger
than my need
          to be right."

"...if you won't be honest
with me
because you're worried
about hurting me...
you'll hurt me
so much more
if i find out
you were being dishonest."

"...i think it's alright
            to be sure...
      but,
            not to be 'so sure'
                  that i think
            i'm always right."

Chapter Two

Being True to Our Heart

...i'm seeing more and more that life is a 'reflection' of how i'm feeling about myself ...To 'grow,' for me, has meant making changes, forgiving myself and others, and staying in touch with the 'child' that i believe is within us all ...i hope this next chapter gives you the support to 'grow' that so many friends have given me, and i hope it leaves you thinking, smiling, and caring more, so we can all live life fully and in peace.

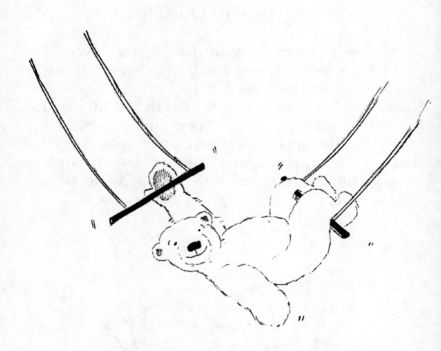

"...when i think
i need to belong,
i often follow others...
when i follow my heart,
i feel i belong,
regardless of others."

"...the most important thing
            for me to remember
      is how unimportant
                  'things' are."

"...i'm not going,
to leave you...
i'm leaving,
to go find me."

"...i'd rather become 'well-known'
            because of the things i do...
than do things
            to become 'well-known'."

"...when we're children
we have limitless imaginations...
when we grow up
we're often limited
by our images."

"...i'm not a human being
                spending a lot of time
        trying 'to become'
                        spiritual...
        i'm a 'spiritual being'
                experiencing the trials
        of being human,
                for a short while."

"...the most unselfish thing
i can do
is to be selfish
about doing
what makes me happy...
it's when i'm happiest
that i give the most
to others."

"...happiness
   isn't being
      all smiles...
happiness
   is knowing
      i can 'be'
      however i 'feel'
         like being."

"...when we're babies,
           we just 'are',
        and we don't worry about
              what we're going 'to be'...
    when we grow up,
           we worry about
        what we're 'going to be',
              and we stop 'being'
        who we 'are'."

"...advice adds another voice
to my head to confuse me...
and gives me
another person to blame
when their advice
doesn't work."

"...i'm not excited
about the challenge
        of winning
            someone else's heart
        so i'll feel good
            for a little while...
    i'm excited
            about the challenge
        of staying in touch
            with my own heart,
    so i'll know how
            to feel good forever."

"...why do we love
       that dogs,
              cats,
                   and flowers,
    are all different colours,
                        kinds,
                             and styles...
    and yet,
       it's those very same qualities
              that separate us so much
          as people?"

"...i want to work hard
on my faults...
but,
be easy on myself
when i falter."

"...by being willing
            to take the risk
                to be different,
    we may find
            that 'deep down'
                we are all the same...
    by trying
            to be the same,
        we are often afraid
                of those
            who may 'appear'
                    different."

"...i'd rather make mistakes
and find out
'who i am'...
than make the mistake
of being afraid,
and always wonder
'who am i'?"

"...future promises
often give me
a false sense
of security...
when i sense
what's false
in the moment,
i become more secure."

"...the more i become
myself...
the more becoming
i become
to others."

"...it takes a lot
  of hard work
 to get a mark...
it takes a lot
  of 'heart' work
 to leave a mark."

Chapter Three

The Courage to Follow Our Heart

...To me life is simple; we've made it complicated, and the challenge is to get back in touch with its simplicity ...i hope, through this next chapter, you're able to see more clearly why i think we lose touch with our hearts, and how we can and need to regain this closeness if we're to experience 'peace within' towards a more 'harmonious world'.

"...i now know that trust
isn't based on
the length of time
i've known someone...
it's how i'm feeling
with someone
at that moment
in time."

"...when we're sensitive
we can believe
we're not strong...
or we can feel strong
by believing in
our sensitivity."

"...if i'm sad about something
        and you don't know what to say...
please don't say anything,
        you'll say so much more."

"...when i worry 'too much
           about how i look',
     i seem to attract 'too many'
         who only care about my looks,
       and it makes me wonder
                 if anyone cares...
     when i care more about
                   how i feel,
           i may only attract a few
                who care about my feelings,
       but i'll get more of the feeling
                     that people do care."

"...it's not changing places
            that will make me change...
    it's the change
            that takes place in me...
    although
        a change of place
                may help that change,
                            in me,
            to take place."

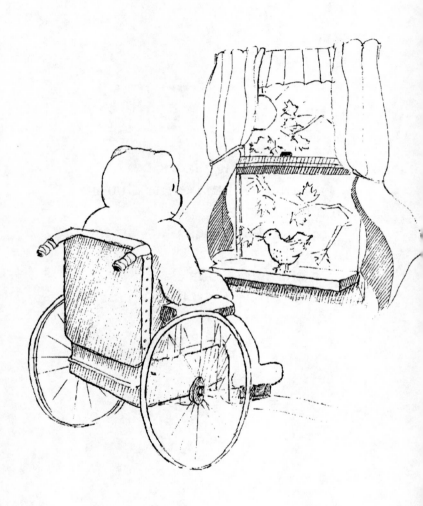

"...if i 'love' someone,
i accept them
however they are...
when i 'want' someone,
i only accept them
if they are
however i want them
to be."

"...as the loving voice
in my heart
is allowed
to come out...
the fearful voices
in my head
stop coming out
so loud."

"...are you saying that
    because you really feel
        that way,
  or because others
        have told you
   that's the way
      you should feel?"

"...peace begins
when i begin
to see
that peace begins
within me."

"...either,
    we are all strangers,
  as i've lived
      with me
  all my life
  and i don't even know
       who i am yet...
or,
   none of us are strangers,
     if we see the beautiful 'essence'
     within everyone...
  it's that 'essence' that we,
    too often,
     have become strangers with."

"...i feel more positive and peaceful
               when i put my energy
         into doing
             what i believe in,
         than when i go 'against'
                       what i don't...
   and i smile
           more often too."

"...as i learn to listen
            to my heart,
      i'm learning
            more and more,
that i need to
      unlearn the fears
            i learned before."

"...i felt negative
            when i thought
      i was a 'victim'...
but really,
            i was only a victim
                  of negative thoughts."

"...when i 'worry' about someone,
i'm not believing in them,
i'm only giving myself power,
and they become weaker...
when i care about someone,
i'm believing in them,
and i'm giving them extra strength
to become stronger."

"...my greatest fear
is that i become afraid
because i listen to
what others think
i should be afraid of."

"...intelligence is
     what i know...
  wisdom is
     what i do
        with what i know...
  awareness is
     knowing why i do
        what i do
           with what i know...
  and happiness is
     'doing' it."

"...i can be hurt
        by others
    in 'all' ways
        except spiritually...
the only way
    i can be hurt spiritually
    is by wanting
        to hurt others,
    in 'any' way."

"...often,
   with choices,
      the hard part
   isn't 'knowing'
         what i should do...
   it's 'doing'
         what i know
            i should do."

The Great Gift

The Great Gift Story

For someone special

Toog and Heather were born at the very same time, on the very same day. Toog was gentle and cuddly and considered himself very smart. He loved to spend time learning and thinking and sharing all his wonderful discoveries with Heather. Heather was kind and caring and constantly surrounded by a warm, loving glow—in fact she was all Heart!

Even though they looked very different, Heather and Toog were best friends and went everywhere together. They were inseparable!

One day, Toog decided he wanted to learn about the outside world. So he packed up all his belongings and jumped on his bicycle. Heather couldn't ride a bicycle, so Toog held her very close to his chest with one paw and steered with the other. He hadn't pedaled very far when someone shouted at him, "Hey! You can't steer a bicycle with only one paw!"

Heather seemed to shrink a little at the sound of the angry voice and Toog felt embarrassed. He stopped and put Heather in a sling on his back. "Now I'm doing it right!" he said. But with Heather behind him, he could no longer hear her kind and quiet voice.

After they had ridden for several miles, they stopped to rest. Some other travelers were also stopping there. They explained to Toog that they were searching for the Great Gift—which was a mysterious something that made life wonderful. They didn't know what or where it was, but they were determined to track it down.

They all looked very fine in their expensive clothes and they rode the most beautiful bicycles Toog had ever seen. They looked at Toog and Heather and began to snicker. "Such a fine looking bicycle and such a fine looking rider, but why have you got that creature strapped to your back? Someone like you would be welcome to join us in our quest—but lose the lump!"

Toog felt proud that the other travelers thought he was good enough to join them. He didn't really want to part with Heather, but he did want to fit in with the rest of the crowd. He was afraid he wouldn't be accepted by them if he remained true to his dear, little friend.

Toog thought and thought. Finally, he got a small wagon and put Heather in it. He attached the wagon to his bicycle by a very long rope and hoped no one would notice Heather tagging along behind. He didn't even see how forlorn and small she looked, sitting all alone at the end of her rope!

His new friends resumed their search for the Great Gift. Toog accompanied them with Heather in tow. Somehow this felt very different from the other times Toog had spent with Heather. For one thing, no one seemed to be having any fun.

"This is a very important venture," he was told by Sigmund, the leader of the group. "Remember, it is vital that we act like the serious and intelligent explorers we are. Those who see us must understand—just by looking—that we are a force to be reckoned with. That way, they will be so impressed they will help us in any way we ask."

Toog put on a serious expression and tried to think important thoughts. He and the other explorers spent hours analyzing and discussing all the Great Gift stories they heard on their travels. When his new friends told Toog that he was very smart, he felt important and proud.

The villagers in the cozy, little villages they traveled through were duly impressed by the group. They asked Toog and the others to stay awhile and help them understand the meaning of the stories about the Great Gift. Even though no one in Toog's group really understood everything, they were pleased to be asked. They spent hours telling the villagers what they thought the Great Gift was and how to find it.

"The Great Gift is Power," one explorer told the crowd. "No, the Great Gift is Wealth," said another. "The Great

Gift is Irresistible Beauty," said a third.

"But how do we find it?" they were always asked.

"The Great Gift can only be found by denying your-self and living alone on top of a mountain," said one. "No, the Great Gift can only be found by accomplishing impossible feats of daring," said another. "You are both wrong," said a third, "The Great Gift is only attained by defeating all your opponents."

Toog wasn't sure about all this, but he didn't want the others to think he couldn't understand, so he pretended to agree with them. When Heather told Toog that none of the answers felt right to her, Toog ignored her and pulled even further away. He thought he knew what Heather's feelings were, but what did they have to do with anything important?

They traveled on with Heather still following at a distance. The others pointedly ignored her and even Toog sometimes wished he didn't have to pay attention to Heather. He often felt mortified by her simple observations and expressions of feeling.

One day, Sigmund called Toog over. "I understand you feel a certain 'attachment' to Heather," he said. "No doubt she was a good friend when you were a cub. Why, even I had someone in my life very much like Heather— but, of course, I outgrew her. It's time you realized that there is no room for Hearts in the serious business of living. They just slow everyone down. Toog, it's time to cut Heather loose!"

Without another thought, Toog reached down and cut the rope. Now he was truly heartless.

Poor Heather. When the wagon finally stopped and she realized what had happened, she felt a terrible pain. Still, she ignored the heartache and set off to follow Toog. She wasn't sure she could catch up, but she loved Toog and she had a feeling he was headed for disappointment. One day soon, Toog would need her, so she just had to continue.

Weeks passed and many, many miles were covered. Toog and his friends looked everywhere, but they never seemed to get any nearer to solving the mystery of the Great Gift. Worse, his new friends had taken to fighting amongst themselves. They bickered and blamed each other for their failure.

One night, discouraged and headachy, Toog sat on a boulder and looked up at the darkened sky. As a falling star flashed overhead, he remembered Heather and all the good times they had enjoyed star-gazing and making wishes. He remembered how good it had felt to be with someone who loved and accepted him just for who he was.

A terrible feeling of loneliness swept over him and he felt his eyes fill with tears. "Oh, Heather," he sighed, "Why didn't I have the courage to keep you with me? My new friends don't make me happy and I'm no closer to finding the Great Gift."

A quiet, well-loved voice answered from behind a nearby bush, "When we think we need to belong, we often follow others—when we follow our Heart, we feel we belong regardless of others."

"Heather!" Toog exclaimed and turned to see her smiling face beaming from behind a branch. Toog rushed up to Heather and caught her in a giant bear-hug. "I'm so glad to see you," he said. "I missed you so much! You're an important part of me. I'll never again pretend that you're not."

"I missed you too," Heather smiled. She stretched up as tall as she could and gave Toog a sweet kiss on the end of his nose. Toog felt the warmth of that kiss right down to his toes, and with it the feeling of being gentle and cuddly returned. Heather smiled again, "Come on, let's go and find the Great Gift!"

"But how?" asked Toog. "The smartest brains have not been able to figure it out— how can we hope to?"

"Silly, old Toog," replied Heather fondly. "The Great Gift is there for everyone, but you can only find it by following your Heart!"

"Why didn't you tell me that before?" Toog asked. "I wanted to," replied Heather, "But you wouldn't listen to me."

"I'm sorry," said Toog. "I'm listening now."

"Well, then, follow me!" laughed Heather and she turned and started off. Toog followed close behind. But Toog wasn't the only one following Heather. As the two friends made their way through the night, another figure followed close behind. It was Sigmund

"I wondered where that Toog fellow was sneaking off to," he thought. "So you have to follow your Heart, eh? If I'd known that, maybe I would've kept mine." He paused for a moment as memories of his own long-lost friend filled his mind. Shaking off the sad, sweet feeling that stole over him, he continued. "Ah, well. What's done is done. The important thing now is that I've got to beat those two to the Great Gift. Otherwise the years I've spent looking for it have been wasted!" Keeping well in the shadows and stepping very quietly, he trailed the reunited friends.

Meanwhile, Toog and Heather were having a wonderful time. Hand in hand they walked, mile after mile, trading memories and funny stories. As dawn broke and the sweet smell of morning filled the air, they took the time to look around and appreciate the beauty of the woods they passed through. They gathered nuts and berries for breakfast and Toog even found some honey for dessert. They enjoyed the songs of the birds and the loving warmth of the sun as it caressed the tops of their heads.

"It's been so long since I felt this happy," thought Toog. "Even if we never find the Great Gift, this journey has been worthwhile!"

After they finished their breakfast, they started off again with Heather still in the lead. After walking most of that day, the woods gradually gave way to a field that was bordered by a road. The road led to a small town filled with creatures who all looked just like Heather! The creatures clustered closely around the newcomers.

"What is this place?" Toog asked. One of the creatures came forward and introduced herself. "I'm Clarissa," she said. "This is a way-station where searchers for the Great Gift can rest and refresh themselves and prepare for the final leg of their journey."

"Are we close?" asked Toog. "Very close," Clarissa replied, "But you still have one more region to pass through before you find it."

"Why do only Hearts live in this village?" Toog inquired.

"Once, we all had friends like you Toog," Clarissa told him, "But one by one they left us, years ago, to follow their ambitions. They mistakenly believed they could find their dreams by going it alone—that taking their Hearts with them would put them at a disadvantage."

"If the ones you loved abandoned you so long ago," Toog queried, "Why aren't you all heartbroken?"

Clarissa laughed. "Because we know that no one can really lose their Heart," she said. "We believe that one day all our loved ones will return to us. When they do, we will be here; ready to lead them to the happiness they've been looking for. There's no reason for us to be sad. We know that courage and patience will eventually bring us our heart's desire."

Toog was amazed at the faith of the little, heart-shaped creatures. He looked at his own dear Heather. "It's true," he said. "Your courage and patience made it possible for us to be reunited, and we'll never be apart again."

The villagers took Heather and Toog to a charming guest house where they could rest. Just as the sun went down, one of their hosts came to Toog and Heather's quarters. On a map painted on a wall, she showed them the route to take to reach the Great Gift. The friends thanked her, unaware that another set of eyes had been watching. Sigmund, who had followed them to the village and hidden nearby, had been peering through their window!

"I've done it!" he chortled to himself. "I know the route. They won't be leaving until morning, but if I start now, I'll get the Great Gift and be gone before anyone else knows about it." He hugged himself with excitement and slipped off into the blackness of the night.

From behind the curtain of a nearby window, Clarissa's startled face stared out. A thoughtful expression came into her eyes, then she smiled a knowing smile.

Morning finally came. Heather and Toog were surprised to see fog shrouding all the houses in the village. "How will we ever find our goal when we can't even see where the path is leading?" worried Toog.

"This is a common occurrence," Clarissa reassured him. "Searchers often encounter fog on the last leg of their journey." She reached up and patted one of Toog's paws in a comforting manner. "Remember Toog, have courage, patience and—above all else—follow your Heart—then you can't help but reach your goal."

Hand in hand, the two friends walked into the fog. At first, Toog felt anxious. This misty, new world seemed strange and unfriendly, but Toog held tightly to Heather's hand and concentrated on courage. "I may not be able to change the world I see around me," he thought, "But I can change the way I see the world within me."

They hadn't gone far when off in the distance they heard the sound of someone crying. Toog wasn't sure whether they should change their route, but Heather insisted on trying to find and help whoever was so upset. They followed the sound of crying and found Sigmund.

"Sigmund!" exclaimed Toog. "What are you doing here?"

"I followed you," Sigmund confessed, "And saw that Heart drawing on the map on your wall. I knew if I didn't leave then, that you would beat me to the Great Gift—and it's mine! I've been searching my whole life for it. I deserve to find it—not some 'Toog-come-lately'!"

"But why are you just sitting here?" Toog questioned.

"It's this awful fog!" wailed Sigmund. "I can't find the right path. I tried and I tried—but I can't! I've been walking all night, and I'm cold and I'm tired, and now I just don't know what to do!"

Heather and Toog looked at each other. A silent conversation seemed to pass between them as they looked at Sigmund and back. "You can come with us," Toog said finally. "We'll share the Great Gift."

"Share," mused Sigmund, while looking at his feet and crossing his fingers behind his back, "Yes, share. All right, you win." With that, the trio set off again.

The fog was even denser now and cold trickles of moisture ran down their bodies, making them feel clammy and miserable. The terrain too seemed more difficult. There were prickly bushes and big boulders to climb over or around at every turn. Finally, they came to a circular area surrounded by a number of scrubby thorn bushes. The fog seemed a little lighter here, and they could see that in the centre of the circle was a well. Carved into the stone surrounding the well, in very large letters that appeared somehow to glow, were the words: "Bring Mind and Heart to Me—The Great Gift You Shall See."

Sigmund and Toog started forward in great excitement. They were both tall enough to step over and around the cruel thorn bushes, but Heather, being small and rotund, just couldn't pass between or over without being poked and scratched.

"Wait for Heather," Toog insisted.

"Not likely," scoffed Sigmund. "She's served her purpose. We don't need her anymore. Come on Toog, don't be a chump! We'll split the Gift between the two of us."

"No," Toog said firmly. "We've come this far, I won't leave Heather now." Toog reached down and picked Heather up. He cradled her tenderly in his arms. "You're worth more to me than anything," he told her. Then, stepping carefully and slowly around the prickly bushes, he followed after Sigmund. When he found Sigmund however, a very different sight met his eyes from what he had expected. Instead of a triumphant and gloating Sigmund, he found a disconsolate and defeated one.

"It's a cheat!" Sigmund groaned. "I looked and there's nothing there! All these years—searching, planning, working so hard to find the Great Gift—and there's nothing there. Don't risk the pain of failure, leave now!"

Heather and Toog looked at Sigmund and then at each other. Could it be? Could they have come all this way for nothing? Gathering up his courage, Toog said to Sigmund, "We'll never find out what we can do, unless we do all we can to find out."

Hesitantly, hand in hand, Heather and Toog approached the well and looked within. All at once the sun burst through and dispersed the remaining fog! Light seemed to come from every direction to bathe and fill Heather and Toog with love. They felt transformed and somehow connected to the Light, to the world around them and to each other, in a new and wonderful way. So much so, that they cried out with Joy! Jointly they realized that in some mysterious fashion, they were a part of the Light of Love.

In the water of the well, they saw their reflection smiling up at them and they realized that the Great Gift was not for Heather or Toog alone, but that "Toog-Heather" (together) they could receive it and share it with the world.

"Wow!" exclaimed Toog, "The Great Gift is us!" Heather continued, "Yes, and only when we have found this truth can we give the Gift of Love."

"But what about me?" wailed Sigmund. Clarissa, who had followed and had been waiting in the shadows, slipped out and took his hand. "Come my old friend," she said. "You left me behind so long ago, but I've been waiting for you. Now join your mind with my heart and we two will go to the well and receive the Great Gift."

Sigmund gave a grateful cry when he recognized his own dear friend. An emptiness deep inside suddenly seemed to fill with joy and relief. He stood straighter and a peaceful expression came over his face. Then, he took Clarissa's hand and together they went to the well and returned transformed.

With happy hearts and minds, the four friends set off on their new journey to share the Great Gift with the world.

So, may we all have the courage to 'get ahead' by following our Heart to Love.

Chapter Four

The Determined Heart

...An essential thing i want you to know in this chapter is that when we go within, we'll never go without 'everything' that is essential.

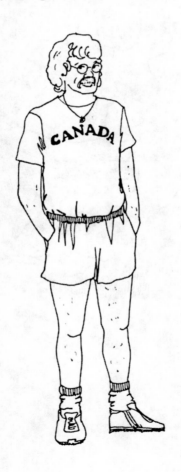

"...i'll never find out
                    what i can do
         unless i do all i can
                              to find out."

"...our happiness
doesn't depend
on the number of challenges
we are handed...
but on how
they are handled."

"...the blind can't see,
how we who see,
can be so blind
to seeing,
that what's most
worthy of seeing,
cannot be seen
by the eye."

"...it's alright
to have opinions,
but not to be
so opinionated
that i always
have to be right."

"...if i don't live in the 'now',
because i'm worried
about my future,
then in the future,
i'll probably be worried
about my future's future...
...if i live in the 'now',
now,
i'll probably be living
in the 'now'
in the future,
and i'll realize that
there was nothing
to worry about,
before."

"...the 'love of power'
            is unloving...
whereas 'to love'
            is empowering."

"...the beautiful thing
            about a mistake,
is that it is no longer
            a mistake
if i learn from it."

"...there is growth
in any
decision...
in indecision
there isn't
any."

"...i'd rather take a risk
        and fail,
    than fail
        to take a risk,
    and always wonder
            what 'if'."

"...when i'm discouraged,
          i only see 'problems',
     and i think i'm dying...
when i'm full of courage
     my problems become 'challenges',
     and it feels good
               knowing i'm living."

"...strength
    isn't 'acting'
        real strong...
strength
    is to quit acting
        and be 'real.'"

"...winning may be doing
         the best time...
but 'winners'
         have the best time
                  doing it."

"...so often,
    we strive to get
the trophies,
      marks,
        and money,
hoping to make ourselves
      feel better,
and maybe even
      to impress others...
and yet,
    when we 'pass on',
the ones who made
    the greatest impression
weren't those
    who cared about
what others' thought,
but were those
    who were the most
thoughtful and cared."

"...success is not 'what' i do
and what others think about it...
success is 'how' i do it,
and that i feel good in my heart
about it."

"...when i'm wise,
i see that my anger
isn't with others...
it's from my expectations
of others,
to be otherwise."

"...i think being on time
           is being thoughtful
     of another 'Being's'
               time."

"...it takes
      courage
  not to be
      discouraged
  from being
    belittled
  when we were
       little."

"...i'm not angry because of my past,
but because i 'hang on to' my past...
when i understand, learn from, and let go
of my past,
the 'past' becomes a wonderful teacher
for appreciating the 'present' more,
in the 'future'."

Chapter Five

The Joyful Heart

...i didn't write these 'thoughts' so you'd feel i've written a beautiful book ...i wrote this book so you'd feel 'your beauty' with each 'thought.'

"...we are given so much
        with the 'gift of life'...
with this gift
        we can give so much
                to others."

"...i want a holiday
            so i'll come back
        and do something about
            the situations
        i need a holiday from...
i don't want a holiday
            just to have a rest
    and come back
            to the situation
        so i'll need another holiday."

"...if you have something nice to say
about me,
please say it to me now
while i'm alive and need it,
not when it's too late
and i'm gone."

"...it's not so important to think
about the things i don't have,
and how to get them...
as it is to appreciate
the things i do have,
and why it's important
not to forget them."

"...the present moment
            is a gift to me...
    my gift
        is to be present
            every moment."

"...i'm not wondering
           where i'm going
      after i die...
i'm going after
           the wonders of living
      while i'm alive."

"...when i thought
        the light
    was at the end
          of the tunnel,
   i got 'tunnel-vision'...
when i see that
      the light's within,
  there's no longer
        any tunnels visible."

"...my 'sole' purpose
            is finding
        my 'soul's' purpose."

"...i don't want to go through
            'the motions' of life...
        i want to live life
            with emotion."

"...so often,
      we take so long
            to look our best
        to take our dog
              for a walk,
and everyone comments
        on what a beautiful dog
      we have."

"...i do 'enjoy'
            things...
    but 'joy'
        comes from loving
            the things i do."

"...i may not be able
        to change the world
   i see around me...
but i can change the way
        i see the world,
   within me."

"...i'm not afraid
            of growing old...
    i'm excited
            about 'growing'
    as i get older."

"...some people love
          to be intelligent
    but they're not necessarily
                              wise...
  a wise person
        appreciates their intelligence,
        but knows
            what's necessary
        is their love."

"...i was told
        i'd be 'out-of-my-mind'
    to go after
            my dreams...
  now,
    that i've gotten
            out of my mind
        by following my heart,
            i'm living my dreams."

"...we are only children
once...
but we can keep the child in us
forever."

"...i'm no longer dreaming
          about how i'd like
     to be living...
  i'm now
       'living the dreams'
     i used to long for."

Chapter Six

The Kind Heart

…This chapter is inspired by those in my life who believe as i do: that we all have beautiful and kind hearts and it's when we lose touch with our heart that we do the not-so-nice things that we too often do.

"...kind words impress...
    kind actions
        leave an impression."

"...every 'Human Being'
         is one-of-a-kind...
to be human
         is to live 'as one'
and be kind."

"...i always love
        to see you...
    but,
        i don't have
            to see you
            to always
                love you."

"...it's easy to love those
who are the most loving,
but what about those
who need love most."

"...the unconditional love
you have shown me
in a moment,
has shown me,
that it 'is' possible to love,
in every moment,
under any condition."

"...we are meant to be
kind humans...
that is why we're called
'Humankind'."

"...when i seek love from others,
          i don't see love in myself...
when i love myself,
          i stop seeking,
and i start to see
          that i only get love
                    by giving."

"...it's nice to
be kind...
but,
being kind
isn't always
being nice."

"...i may be
        passionate about
            what i believe in...
        but i believe
            i need to be
        compassionate
            with those
        who have
            other beliefs."

"...there are a lot
of 'home'less people
living in big houses."

"...i saw a group of blind people
                crossing the street,
        helping each other,
                    laughing,
            and openly showing
                    warm feelings
        towards each other...
they were all different
            ages, colours, and styles of dress...
    it didn't seem to influence
                their caring for each other...
    i couldn't help wondering
                'who' is really blind."

"...i may not always believe
            what you say and do....
    but,
        i can always say,
            i do 'believe in' you."

"...being special
       isn't necessarily
   doing things
         differently...
it's finding it
     necessary
   that the things
         we do
    make a difference."

"...i'm not reliable
        just to the people
    i like better...
i'm reliable
        to all people
    so i'll like myself
            better."

"...what i get most
         from you,
      is not what you give
                  to me...
   it's what i get,
        from seeing how much
            you give to others."

"...one kind act
by one kind person
is the kind of action
that shows kindred spirits
how kindness
can rekindle
our oneness."

"...we're called
         'Human Beings'
because
            'being human'
    is our calling."

"...even though
  you're in my presence
          too little...
  you're in my thoughts
          a lot...
and
  you're in my heart
          always."

Chapter Six

"A Final Thought from Brock"

i hope these "thoughts" and the "story" i've written from my heart connect with, and touch your heart, and inspire you to go inward and see that you, and we, are all special and kind in our essence - as Eckhart Tolle shows, so clearly and wisely, in his books, The Power of Now and The New Earth.

i believe that we need to, then, "come out of ourselves," reach out, and be of service in our communities, and i also believe that our reaching out through simple acts of kindness will ripple globally and transform the world by creating healthy loving communities. There, we will see the importance of volunteering and being involved as an essential part of our heart's journey toward creating a kinder, more loving world.

A friend, Anita, at fourteen, said to me over thirty years ago something that has stayed with me profoundly, and has inspired me to this day: "Brock, you know that beautiful saying, 'live each day as if it's your last!' Wouldn't it be great if everyone lived each day as if it is the last day for everyone they meet?!"

By taking action every day in very simple, but powerful ways, we can each make a huge positive difference, like so many inspiring people have done - Gandhi, Martin Luther King, the Dalai Lama, Mother Teresa, globally, and locally in Vancouver, Terry Fox, Rick Hansen, and many, many others who are unsung, everyday heroes.

A simple thing we can all do to make a positive difference- next time we go for a walk, jog, run, bicycle, or scooter ride, let's "come out of ourselves," reach out, and say a simple "hi" to passersby – we might just turn around someone's day or even their life, and most likely our own as well, and we will be more likely to see, smell, hear, and "feel" the wonders of nature that surround us.

Author Biography

After a 10,000 mile bicycle journey around North America, Brock Tully wrote his first 'thought.' This initial trip was followed by two more internationally publicized bicycle tours: "Cycling for Kindness" in 2000 and "Cycle it Forward" in 2009. Both aimed at raising awareness about the value of kindness. Today Tully is an internationally renowned speaker and author of eight books. In addition to his "Reflections" book series, he is the co-founder of the Kindness Foundation of Canada, which has created on-line programs on how kindness can be fostered at school, at work and at home. He is the founder/creative director of the World Kindness Concert and co-founder of Kindness Rocks in Schools—to prevent bullying, and the abuse of animals and nature. He is also the founder/producer of One of a KIND Stories.

Brock Tully shares thought-provoking, heart-warming, and fun multi-media keynote presentations (and workshops) at conferences, businesses, schools, and other group settings. As a speaker, he includes inspiring stories and insights from his three epic bicycle journeys around North America to raise awareness for a kinder world.

To learn more about Brock Tully please visit
www.brocktully.com

Brock Tully's other books:

"Reflections...for someone special"
"Reflections...for living life fully"
"Reflections...for touching hearts"
"Reflections...for sharing dreams"
"Reflections...for the kind soul"
"With Hope We Can All Find Ogo Pogo"
"The Great Gift"
"Coming Together...a 10, 000 mile bicycle journey"

Contributing Author for:
"HEARTMIND WISDOM Collection #1"
"The Thought That Changed My Life Forever"

If you want to get on the path to be a published author by **Influence Publishing** please go to **www.InspireABook.com**

Inspiring books that influence change

More information on our other titles and how to submit your own proposal can be found at **www.InfluencePublishing.com**

CPSIA information can be obtained at www.ICGtesting.com
Printed in the USA
LVOW08s0712061013

355500LV00002B/20/P